Figure Study

Figure Study

by Kathryn de Lancellotti

**MOON
TIDE PRESS**

~ 2024 ~

Figure Study
© Copyright 2024 Kathyrn de Lancellotti
All rights reserved. No part of this book may be used or reproduced in any manner whatsoever without written permission from either the author or the publisher, except in the case of credited epigraphs or brief quotations embedded in articles or reviews.

Editor-in-chief
Eric Morago

Editor Emeritus
Michael Miller

Marketing Specialist
Ellen Webre

Proofreader
Jeremy Ra

Front cover art
David Shannon

Author photo
Kori Savoie

Book design
Michael Wada

Moon Tide logo design
Abraham Gomez

Figure Study
is published by Moon Tide Press

Moon Tide Press
6709 Washington Ave. #9297
Whittier, CA 90608
www.moontidepress.com

FIRST EDITION

Printed in the United States of America

ISBN # 978-1-957799-25-4

Contents

Root	10
Find Me	12
I was told	14
The Astronaut and the Suit	15
I Didn't Train Hard Enough to Be an Astronaut (Nor a Mother)	18
Water Song	20
Whale Song	21
We Ate the Fruit in Season	22
What God Is	24
Lake Drift	25
Homage to My Period	35
These Walls	36
The Meadowlark	37
I learned young:	38
Rain Song	39
A Daughter's Grief	40
Yael's Tent: A Recurring Childhood Dream	41
Moving Day	42
We Were Young	44
Oval Window	45
There's nothing lonelier	46
Emily Dickinson Got Me Thinking (About God)	47
Local Beach, California	48
American Girl in Italy, 1951	49
The Boot	50
That Bay, I Swear, It Has Become Me	51
Let's sit together	53
Figure Study	54
In Father's house	60
Not to the Father Will I Give Myself	61
Veil of the Flower	62
Social Work	63
Things We Do	65

Delilah	74
Farewell: Eaten by Dogs	75
Remember Me	76
Dust dissolves	77
The World's Broken	78
Cypress Cemetery	80
Last Life	81
Solar Flare	83
About the Author	*85*
Acknowledgements	*86*

*It's not some pilgrim who claims to have seen the Light/
No, it's a cold and it's a very broken Hallelujah.*

— Leonard Cohen

Root

Moonlight in the kitchen is a sign of God.

— Anne Carson

A redwood falling is a sign of God

is a boy who discovers
his father's homeless

wants to feed every
hungry mouth

on every hungry corner.
A tree feeding its sapling

to reduce root competition
for the next generation

is a sign of God.
When a redwood

fell across Cold Springs Ct.
and blocked the road

to Planned Parenthood
a woman listened—

she was stuck in a storm
and it took days to slice

the trunk away.
Two days too late

is a sign.
Is a dying tree

sending wisdom to its kin
sending carbon

signals for defense.
The forest

not a tangled mess
of competition—

but a mother reaching
for a star, rooting

into darkness
is a sign of God

is wet soil,
that final place—

God's mouth
just waiting to swallow.

Find Me

A voiceless flower/speaks/to the obedient/in-listening ear.

   — *Onitsura*

Find me on my back
watching sky
through castor leaves in spring–

in Shadow Canyon
the atmospheric rivers, bomb
cyclones have left–

the tiger swallowtail appeared.
Find me in the swimming hole
ice cold. Watch my nipples

erect, watch me dip
my face in holy waters
watch a woman's head go under.

Find me soaking sunlight
in my mouth, watch me watch
my lover aroused.

Watch the peacock, the cows, elk
in the middle of the road.
Find me naked

in the canyon, find it clearing
out the old, watch the live oak
fall on the Tacoma–

feel my heartbeat
hold me river
guide me. Find me

in the orchard eating
Golden Delicious
watch me

birth in groundwater
spread open.
Watch a face appear
as I scream.
Find me righteous pain, piercing
joy, my daughter at my tit.

The storms are over
California's still in drought.
Find me in the garden

eating radish, praising dirt.
Find me voiceless in the river
lupine my listening ear.

I was told

the entrance to my body was not beautiful

The Astronaut and the Suit

1

My body, you're an animal
a bloody animal.

Before I left my mother
we made an agreement.

You promised to hold me.
I promised to feed you.

My body, you're the door
my son entered and left.

You grew him
with the discipline of a Rishi

and the efficiency of a watch.
I'm starving but I can't eat

my body, I burn toast
to swallow black.

Chew and chew and chew.

2

My body you're bone
and germ, rain soak and bruise.

A mirror of ancestors,
a pain map. You pushed

my children
from soft, torn meat.

You're the thing
I talk to the thing I hate.

I can hardly eat. I'm so full–
why does life have to ache?

You're the rock on the hillside
the lone lamb drinking from the lake.

3

My body you're dust
and blue
a dinner plate wound.
You grew
children
fed them—
antibodies, milk, blood
pleasure seed.
Skin to skin
my daughter
in your eyes.

I Didn't Train Hard Enough to Be an Astronaut (Nor a Mother)

I forgot what it's like to breathe in this suit:

                                                Is it true

                                              attachment

                                  is the root of suffering

                                          without it

                                we have nothing to lose?

I forgot how lonely–

how earth

is a dew drop

how small I've become

far from home

lost

in what's above but feels below

such expanse

                                      Blue is more a feeling

                         a way for the eye to comprehend

                                                      sky

I didn't train hard enough—

they don't tell you how the pressure

is painful

how your heart

could literally break

                                         It sounds so simple

                                                detach—

                                    as if the cord is not your lifeline

                                    as if you're not alone in outer space

Water Song

The first time my son walked, he ran into the ocean.
I think he was trying to go home
or at least someplace closer.

Whale Song

Did I tell you I found a whale fetus wrapped in seaweed?
Did I tell you the sockets were empty?
It was on a Monday.
The storm split a redwood in two and blocked
the road to Planned Parenthood.
Can you hear the orca sing?
The cries of the dying. She carried her dead calf
for seventeen days before releasing it.
Did I tell
you how waters break?
How fatherless sons pray?
Did you know I unraveled the unborn whale
and stuffed it in my pocket?
Did you know the salmon are disappearing,
the whales are hungry, and the mother pushed
the calf a thousand miles with her head?

We Ate the Fruit in Season
After Jane Hirshfield's "My Life"

My breasts
were the size
of handfuls
golden pears.

My vagina
the size of my son.
Table grapes, wild
almonds, figs

were eaten by codling moths.
I faced the sky
with my eyes,
the nights

with my thighs.
The river rushed
the size of a river.
I wanted nothing

to turn to nothing
to everything

It was my life:

the tea kettle's whistle
the elderberry housing the quail
the Psalms' lost lamb
shaking in the shadow.

My tears were the size
of a mother's, my womb
boundless, burden—nipples
calloused cream.

My hands were the size
of my lover's soft cock.

His seed was the size
of his seed.

We ate the fruit in season
when clusters fell from the trees.

What God Is

I don't want to hear what God is
from a book or a capitalist.
A bearded man on a spiritual quest
or from a pulpit.
I don't want to hear about sin
or that desire leads to suffering.
I want a God who is Tantric
moves slow from toe to crown.
One who appears in fire, in lotus
and between breaths.
I want a God who watches
from as far as Sirius, close as skin—
bright star, obsidian.
I want a God who is an artist
a woman, a man. One who labors
and bleeds, suckles on the afterbirth.
I want a God small enough
to watch the sun fall
into the Pacific.
To climb a eucalyptus
to ravage a wild blackberry.
A God who takes pride in skinning
the mule deer, finds pleasure
in its helpless sway.
I want God to walk down
the golden staircase
for a taste
of this delicious hell.

Lake Drift

You with your precious eyes, you're blind to the corruption of your life.

    — *Tiresias, Oedipus Rex*

When the ophthalmologist
told me I have a vertical misalignment
double vision, she said

the brain will compensate
to keep things straight

It all started to make sense—

The axis of my life tilted
The center divider, me
crawling from the driver's widow

Two scarred faces
in the mirror
letters floating off the page

Things you never tell your kid:
suicidal thoughts, vodka, Valium

how you cry
when you realize you're awake

My boy read *Oedipus Rex* at school today—
Was it familiar when he entered the place she birthed him?
Did his father's blood land like a kiss?

Why do they lie to him?

When he found
his mother
slightly

swaying
by the neck

he had no eyes, only fingers
to read her wrists

I told my love
He'll never understand
aching thighs, blood clots
the weight—

Mothers lie too

Aren't dreams the places
we go when we can't
face the truth?

I dreamt
my son dead
at the bottom of a lake—

I could not reach him, I swear
I could not wake up—

Son,

Did you know
when he took the brooches
that held her robes

and stabbed his eyes
because he couldn't bear the truth
that losing them would only make him see again?

Homage to My Period

Each month
lovers bleed from me.
It hurts, every time
reminds me that love is this:
more flush and death.
Witness unfertilized eggs
droplets of red in a bowl of milk.
Witness the tissue of your unborn spill out.
A cycle, always back to this:
in prayer nine times a day.
This ache in the belly each time
my son asks about his dad.
Each clot I pass
fills the cup full, the cup empty.
It's how the story always goes.

These Walls

One day these walls will become
too full and fall to the floor
like the tick that drank its belly red
and dropped from the dog's ear.
There are invisible webs in every corner
I would have never seen
if not for the black hairs caught
like flies to poison.
I placed my ear to the wall, bees hummed
beneath layers of wallpaper, decades
smoothed over with floral and textures.
When the exterminator smoked the hive
it fled through the chimney—
an angry cloud over Wagon Wheel Blvd.
The milk, the honey, chamomile, Xanax, weed.
I tried everything. My doctor said
If you can't sleep, clean.
I didn't take his advice.
Instead, I lie in bed awake and listen
to my son's breathing.
To owl song and cat fight.
I drift with the night blooming jasmine
into half-dream—
frantically eating my way out
of silk and night, with no choice
but wings
and piercing light.

The Meadowlark

I feel guilty picking lavender
and stepping on stones.
I see a ladybug land in my son's hair
and let it rest awhile.
A long-legged spider weaves a home into the corner.
A reoccurring dream
of a recluse in my bed, I try to kill it with a shoe
but it gets me first.
I'm the one the mosquitoes want to drink
the sucker for love, the meat.
I see a cloud and think I could live here
the sun is peeking through the pine
the vine is climbing the trunk.
We all need a host to carry us.

Sometimes I cry to the lark.
Sometimes I beg for its wings.

I learned young:

run girl, run

Rain Song

I thought I'd try to fly. Thought birds
were angels in disguise

thought God protected his children.
All those nights,

Mother would lie in bed and tremble—
a daisy in a gale, a hummingbird. Sometimes

I hear her scream. She hated when I climbed
the eucalyptus. *Like a bird*, Mother said,
small bones. Like a bird, torn feathers. Bones, broken

so many places—a bird
born to touch the edge of air. Once

driving in the rain on Highway 1
I hit a horned buck—watched it rise
from the pavement and walk into the shrubs. I remember

light through the window. Glass in the gums. Wondered
did the animal search the briar for its ilk?

Today
I woke to what I thought
was Mother, those usual moans:

This is what the rain has become.

A Daughter's Grief

Sylvia,

Aren't we all looking for a way out of the owl's talons?
A way not to remember
the honeybee's sting, the shape of a boot on your back,
all the nights your breasts would leak, a child,
the sucking, the screaming.
Aren't we all looking for a way not to remember
the poems that cry us to sleep, the little ghosts
we carry in our hands, dare we tell?
Forget the Ativan, the razor, your car in Little River.
You wrote in blood, and for your sacrifice, I thank you,
dear Poet, dear Mother, you took care of your children
the best you could. I've heard the stories.

You'd swear no gas seeped through the door.
You'd swear you sealed worlds between us.

Yael's Tent: A Recurring Childhood Dream

The priest asked for water
I gave him milk.
He asked for a place to rest

I gave him a pillow.
When he twitched in dreams
I reached for the peg and hammer—

There, at my feet he sank.
There, in my bed, he was dead.

Moving Day

Is a cul-de-sac in pine trees

My best friend's
Tire swing

Is Father writing
Sermons

Mother baking
Whole wheat

Is Shante asleep
Under the fir tree

Is the gypsy wagon
The Double Decker

Big Wheels
Roller hockey

Bare feet in nasturtiums
Red Rover on the asphalt

Is family
By the wood burning stove

Is popcorn
With sliced apples

Sunsets on the trampoline
Is Shante dead

Under Leslie's car
Buried

By the water tower
Dug up

By coyotes
Is my parents:

"We're sorry"

Is my room empty
Is Hobie on my lap

In the back seat
Is Laura running behind

Father driving
The U-Haul

Sister
Unforgiving

Brother sleeping
Mother speaking—

Is the ocean disappearing?

We Were Young

Remember that thou art dust, and to dust thou shalt return.

— *Genesis 3:19*

We were young
when we left the city lights

to climb the mountain and discover
the tree house was too small for us.

Four redwood pillars couldn't hold the fire
so, I continued to live

without my skin. Red bark burned
through starless nights

coyotes screamed, blue jays
squawked in cypress. I moved

high up the mountain
hoping to feel the hand of God

smear the ash between my eyes,
wash me clean in a silent river.

But the land was broken
and the groves, our first temples

burned. We were banished
by flames, so we climbed down

the mountain, watched ash turn to dust
and float away in the light.

Oval Window

I saw a red-bellied finch
with strands of auburn hair in its beak
watched it tangle dead cells into nest, wildly
weave me into home. My reflection captured
in stained glass—

saw Mother living in my skin, heard Father
say my face could take me places
noticed the way eyes never age.

I filled a bath, left a bowl of seed.
The bird hovered then flew away.

I thought of Sacred Heart Elementary—
how we were taught to pray for a husband.
How the kids laughed at the pretty girl
the day her canary died during show and tell.
No one felt bad for her.
We were taught to pity the girl with leg braces
told she doesn't stand a chance without a man.

I watched the mother bird dive
towards an approaching male.

There's nothing lonelier

than knowing we're made of stars

Emily Dickinson Got Me Thinking (About God)

I saw a bobcat bathing in the middle of a path. She looked
up at me with black eyes and puffed her tail. I got anxious,
yelled, *I love you kitty!*

                My cousin and I were smoking a joint at Thousand Steps
                              when a humpback breached
                          high above the water, then vanished.

I was kayaking topless at Santa Margarita Lake
and without warning, a white-headed eagle
swooped beside me. I screamed
and held both breasts.

                              As I was cooling my sister's forehead,
                                  they broke her waters with a hook
                                    pulled a boy from her womb.

I dreamt I was drinking tea with Emily Dickinson.
She whispered,
the mushroom is the elf of plants.

Local Beach, California

At the end of the beach there's a small cove
surrounded by eucalyptus and coastal sage.
Only locals know it's a nude beach.
Tourists walk by searching for jade
pretending not to look

*

When my grandmother was young
she'd sunbathe naked in the cove.
Mother and I inherited sunlight on our nipples

*

As a child, I'd walk barefoot
through the grove
on a path
of smooth leaves—
climb the cliffs
and watch pelicans dive for fish

*

There's a giant tree in the grove
my brother named Enchanted.
Its limbs stretch out
like the open hands of God.
We'd lie in its fingers, imagine
we were the first people on earth

*

Otters crack shellfish on their chests
while a pod of humpbacks spray sea

*

Clouds pass over my naked body

American Girl in Italy, 1951
After Kim Addonizio's "What Do Women Want?"

(The photo hung above the toilet in a golden frame)

She seemed to move in slow motion
across the old stone sidewalk

clutching her shawl, trying to pass
the corner café, leave behind

fifteen sets of eyes.
Even then I understood

her quickening pulse
the man on the motorbike

checking out her ass, the shameless
one grabbing his crotch.

I've walked that ancient street,
in that black dress

to open mouths spitting red
wine, past tongues

whistling, truck drivers
flashing porno mags.

The photo confirmed my place—
those strappy sandals

that street
all those eyes I wear

like bones, like skin
I pull from the hanger, unzip.

The Boot
After Sharon Olds' "Sex Without Love"

*Every woman adores a fascist, /the boot in the face/the brute/
brute heart of a brute like you.*

    — *Silvia Plath*

I fucked Professor on my period. Pulled his ears
while he plucked the string out with his teeth.
Told me he wasn't afraid to taste a little blood.

I fucked Father on the church pew.
Hymns torn, almost to nothing—how sweet
the sound. How sweet the blood of the lamb.

How do they do it? Sharon asks,
the ones who make love without love?

I tell her I've done it. Done it on dorm room
carpet. Done Daddy next to Jesus, so many daddies
and false Messiahs. I'm not saying it was beautiful

as ice skaters whirling ice, or bones bowed
inside each other. Think crown of thorns.
Think rust and screw. Think I'm ugly

for punishment, that sometimes a daughter
sticks her head in the oven. Sometimes she comes
to the rock for the slaughter, comes face red as wine, red

as meat, red as a child begging *Daddy,
Daddy don't leave.*

That Bay, I Swear, It Has Become Me

I've been the gull
attacked in air

Felt breath disappear—
hooked a bass

swallowed sperm
the way pelicans

slurp sardines
stripped down

for a stranger
south

of the sleeping volcano
—screamed

molten lava
while it surged

Morro Rock.
I've been bedrock

sacrificed my body
to the brine—

wore fracture
on the outside

I taste of sea,
cold saline, birthed

from the pussy
of a clam.

I've been the pale ray
in flight

the chill
of coastal nights

Let's sit together

in the silence, in the dark

Figure Study

1

I was so used to men staring
I thought it was the price I paid.

2

I used to wear fear like a robe I couldn't drop
before walking on stage, afraid
the artist might capture something I can't see
in my own body or face.
I once stood naked in the middle of a classroom
blood dripping between my legs.
I did not move, did not wipe it away.
I let it fall to my feet until the timer rang.

3

I learned to stand naked for hours in stillness
to be the canvas, blank.
To give to the artist what's needed
mostly shadows and shapes.
A man once told me
I was too beautiful to paint, that there was something
about me he couldn't capture.
I learned at a young age not to give it all away
that it's better to be muse than mate.
I told him, I felt the same. I can't grasp myself, either,
too good at silence, at restraint.
I'm an artist, I say, the world is too loud
the body's never still, always churning, bleeding to create.
I want to tell you what it's like
to be cut into marble, hung in a gallery,
frozen in a frame. I want to tell you
what it's like to watch a man mold you in still life
to let him believe he's your maker as he carves
your ivory waist.
Such desire for the body he has formed.
Such art his hands crave—I want to tell you
what it's like to hold a man in stillness, for hours,
then walk out unscathed.

4

Sometimes, I'm clay formed
into his image, flesh-toned oil
on canvas, a photograph, a brush stroke.
Sometimes, model X, subject,
childless, a child
hunched over on the couch
hips holding the weight of frailty.
Here, in this frame
I don't own my body,
I'm kindling burnt off in the pyre.
When I drop my robe
in the middle of the classroom,
or on the floor of the studio
or to the corner of a bed
I give myself to the mystery
to the art
and he takes her
and makes her his own
each vertebra, each bone
and shade, a mirror
he has chased—
a frightened spine
like an arrow through the heart.

5

The body is not
a body

but a looking glass
an empty cup.

The painter gives the rose
eternal life.

We fall in love
with the idea and walk

hallway after hallway
gazing into mirrors

into slow,
certain death.

Pluck a rose
from the garden

place her in a frame.
Watch

pink petals fall
to the floor

remember
the thrill of her

spread open
for you

the fragrance
face to face

with a flower
in bloom

before it breaks.
Remember the body

is not a body
but a shadow
a shape
the model takes.

In Father's house

there's only one way out

Not to the Father Will I Give Myself

Not to confessionals, nor banks, nor country.
I will not drop bombs, will not build walls.

No longer will I give myself to bearded musicians
nor salty surfers. Touch myself instead.

I will not treat Earth the way you treat the feminine.
Will not pour oil into oceans, starve the sacred

polar bear, nor steal ivory from an elephant's face.
It's true, Officer, I told my toddler not to trust you

that you're a dog off leash. Leaders of War,
Money, Pussy grabbing, you may not kiss me

nor choose for me.
I don't pray to Archangel Michael anymore.

I pray to the Mother, to Mary, and to the other Mary.
Dare I say her name?

Washed his feet with her hair—
Saint Magdalene, teach us to love our clitorises.

Teach us multiple orgasms,
no more faking. Teach us to say, no

I don't want to have sex with you
don't want to make your bed. Go ahead, call me a whore.

You've been hurt, too, little brother,
told to take off your sunflower dress.

Veil of the Flower

I found Father face down
in chrysanthemum.

Can't stop seeing his bald head

the quarter moon
the blue sky.

Can't stop the odor

trapped gophers
fried hair.

This is love, I tell myself

a dead Father
finally dead. I didn't cry

didn't bury him in a casket.
I placed a sheet over the rot

and watered with gasoline.
Lit the outline

of a sunflower, offered it
like a lamb.

Social Work

Grandfather has Alzheimer's, every day
his mother died yesterday, and he's always
going home tomorrow. His leg's black,
the infection creeping into his blood
and heart. He refuses amputation; wants
to die with both feet.

The television blaring clips
of the debate, he looks up
from his application, yells,
I hope he kicks her ass!
I don't try to explain his pathetic signature,
that he's signing for socialized medicine
or that his VA pension isn't enough.

The nurse changes his weeping cloths
and doses him with Seroquel to slow
the tremors, to keep him from jumping
out of his wheelchair to escape
the fluorescent halls of his suffering,
the closed doors. He can't remember
his mother's name, but knows the year
the war started, and the exact number
of civilian casualties in Okinawa: 142,058.

I see it every day in these places: ghosts
spoon fed orange Jell-O and Fox news,
haunting the hallways with bags of urine,
begging to be free.

There's talk of the old dying off, of a new
generation seeking tolerance and relief.
I think of ways to end the pain—slide
the white curtain to the edge of to his bed.
Lay a pillow on his face, gently asphyxiate
until the end of an age. Tell him,
    The war's over, go home.
His hands tremble, rise—red poppies
open in the night. A child reaches
for his mother, again.

Things We Do

1

Find a coat hanger deep
inside the closet
Fish out every seed

2

Stick a metal rod
in the mouth
to save the tongue

3

Mutilate the clitoris—
prepare for the feast

4

Dance
until the head
of a prophet is served
on a silver platter

5

Asks
pours
drinks
wants more
takes

6

Hears God demand
a first born
replace a lamb

7

Do you know what he does to his children?
Think you can run someplace he can't?

8

Needed the money
got naked
tied a lover
to a chair
cut his hair

9

Here, it's always winter—
fresh powder covers the stains

Delilah

The first time I bound him,
he begged for it

I took seven ropes
and tied him to a chair

The second time:
chains, a blindfold, a feather—

What's your secret?

The last time,
I poured; he drank

Farewell: Eaten by Dogs
After a 19th-century painting by John Liston Byam Shaw, "Jezebel, Queen of Israel"

Whoever wrote the Bible wanted me remembered
as the Whore of Israel.

They must have hated something I knew or possessed
to give me that title.

I'm not a fighter like Deborah or devoted
like Miriam or nameless like Potiphar's wife.

I didn't steal strength for a haircut,
bathe naked on a rooftop or laugh at God.

Each time I spread my legs
I knew exactly what I was doing.

I've known since the first finger,
the first fist, all the fissures

and tarring and tears. The king's dead,
they killed my son, too.

I won't hide.
I'll stare out the window

and take it. I don't care
what they do with my name,

or with the body
I've already left.

Remember me with a pink rose in my red hair,
eyes lined with kohl.

Remember Me

the blue baby
on the sand
the mother who weeps?
I'm the one who changed—
plucked the fruit
made love to a snake.
Sold my body
absorbed poison in the factory
hid in the desert for days.
I look in the mirror
see nothing.
Can't make a living
or leave.
I'm Sarah laughing at God.
The virgin who birthed kings.
I hold a small hand
spread butter and jam
stuff the freezer full of meat.
I've seen ovaries eaten—
breast sliced open.
I'm the one who bleeds.
There are mornings I cry
others I sing—

I'm the rye rising in the kitchen
drinking the sunlight and the yeast.

Dust dissolves

but never disappears

The World's Broken

I can't help but stare at that sunbeam
through the canopy.

I can't stop writing this poem.

The world's broken yet I marvel
at the flame's magnificence

how it warms to the bone.
How I can't stop looking at my phone—

children buried alive.
I want to fix what's broken:

stitch together Mother's heart
Father's wounded mind.

I want to make the world better—

I can't help but stare at that shadow
in the canyon

the refraction of light
the shattered fawn's cry into night.

The world's full of orphans

but I don't have the energy
for more children. I'm too tired

to take care of them,
to explain

another school shooting
another species dying.

I stare into the vastness
of my daughter's eyes—

tuck my son into bed
tell him he's safe.

Sometimes, the live oak falls
and the road washes away, still

I can't help but notice the wild grasses

early this year—
the well that never went dry.

Cypress Cemetery

Black birds graze
in rows between headstones.
Yellowing grass sways
with westerly winds.
From a broken pine,
starling sing, and I
walk with the dead underneath—
as vultures winnow
in circles over me.

As if I'm the only
one here—slowly dying.

Last Life
An Homage to Caésar Vallejo and Tony Hoagland

I must be close to my last life by now.
The storm has cleared

and the sun's warming my face
through the window—

primal and satisfying
like a cup of broth.

Can a place become a part of you?

Not in the metaphorical way
but in the way clouds

come together and break apart
take position inside of me

become an allegory.
And from this window

I can see what has brought us here—
how sky and earth make love

and where they touch
we're born into these landscapes,

these stories.
But there are stories within stories.

And when I look up
there are questions within questions.

What is God

but the salt I carry on my feet?
Or the I who softly speaks?

When my work here's done
I'll drift with deciduous leaves—

like Vallejo in Paris with a rainstorm.
It will be in Autumn, on a Thursday.

Solar Flare

To discover how to be human now. Is the reason we follow this star.

— *Auden*

The flare wasn't aimed directly towards Earth,
NASA just released.

The largest solar flare in recorded history.
There's a magnetic swirl

of iron and molten
larger than the world's oceans

protecting us from radioactive particles
entering Earth.

We all have fields.
It's vulnerable

to stand on two feet, brains
facing the sky, mutants

in this atmosphere, afraid
to be the first to die.

Seneca said luck is when
preparation and opportunity meet.

Just last week I packed
emergency supplies:

a solar radio, batteries,
flashlights, lentils, rice, canned

peaches, his hands. How
my lover cups my breast,

carries our daughter, holds
my son when he cries.

As far as NASA knows
the field's been thinning, *rapid changes.*

The Aurora Borealis are born
charged particles, radioactive material

colliding with oxygen—
toxic silk lapping the poles.

If it's up to luck
the sun will belch just enough

for us to stay the night
to dream

under green sky, while our cores thump
and burn away.

About the Author

Kathryn de Lancellotti's chapbook *Impossible Thirst* was published June 2020, Moon Tide Press. She's a Pushcart Prize and Best of the Net nominee, and a recipient of the George Hitchcock Memorial Poetry Prize. Her poems have appeared in *Thrush, Rust + Moth, The Night Heron Barks, The American Journal of Poetry,* and others.

Acknowledgements

The author would like to thank the editors of the following publications, in which these poems first appeared, sometimes with a different title:

Audacious Woman Anthology: "American Girl in Italy, 1951"
Audacious Woman Anthology: "Oval Window"
Ballast Journal: "Find Me"
Bending Genres: "Solar Flare"
Bending Genres: "Whale Song"
Catamaran Literary Reader: "Emily Dickinson Got Me Thinking (About God)"
Chicago Quarterly Review: "Local Beach, California"
Chinquapin: "We Were Young"
Cultural Weekly: "Farewell: Eaten By Dogs"
Cultural Weekly: "Not to the Father Will I Give Myself"
Cultural Weekly: "These Walls"
Lady/Liberty/Lit: "Things We Do"
Rabid Oak: "Remember Me"
Red Wheelbarrow: "Oval Window"
Rise Up Review: "A Daughter's Grief"
Rust + Moth: "Figure Study 1,2,3"
Softblow: "The Boot"
Softblow: "Figure Study 4"
Softblow: "Homage to My Period"
Softblow: "The Astronaut and the Suit"
Sounds of the Sandwich Kingdom 2 (cassette): "This Bay, I Swear, It Has Become Me"
Sky Island Journal: "Lake Drift"
Sky Island Journal: "Last Life"
The American Journal of Poetry: "Social Work"
The Night Heron Barks: "Rain Song"
The Shore Poetry: "Meadowlark"
Thrush Poetry Journal: "Root"
Typishly: "Veil of the Flower"
West Trade Review: "We Ate the Fruit in Season"

I would like to thank my love for our beautiful life together and for being the most fun-loving dad to our children. David, thank you for being so damn talented and handsome and cool and for teaching me how to be a better writer and a better human. You still give me butterflies. I love you so much.

Jade and Avalon, my children, my teachers, my mirrors, my heartache, my exhaustion, and my inspiration, thank you for choosing me to be your mom. You're the real poetry—and I love you with my whole being.

To some of the poets who have taught me, encouraged me, and inspired me, thank you: Laura Wetherington, Luke Johnson, Lee Herrick, Gary Young, Alexis Rhone Fancher, Eric Morago, Rich Ferguson, Gayle Brandeis, June Sylvester Saraceno, Shaun Griffin, Patricia Smith, Laura McCullough, Brian Turner, Matt Fleming, and Connie Post.

And thank you, dear reader, for plunging into the cold waters and soaking in the sunlight with me. To share my art with you is pure joy.

Also Available from Moon Tide Press

Suffer for This: Love, Sex, Marriage, & Rock 'N' Roll,
    Victor D. Infante (2024)
What Blooms in the Dark, Emily J. Mundy (2024)
Fable, Bryn Wickerd (2024)
Diamond Bars 2, David A. Romero (2024)
Safe Handling, Rebecca Evans (2024)
More Jerkumstances: New & Selected Poems,
    Barbara Eknoian (2024)
Dissection Day, Ally McGregor (2023)
He's a Color Until He's Not, Christian Hanz Lozada (2023)
The Language of Fractions, Nicelle Davis (2023)
Paradise Anonymous, Oriana Ivy (2023)
Now You Are a Missing Person, Susan Hayden (2023)
Maze Mouth, Brian Sonia-Wallace (2023)
Tangled by Blood, Rebecca Evans (2023)
Another Way of Loving Death, Jeremy Ra (2023)
Kissing the Wound, J.D. Isip (2023)
Feed It to the River, Terhi K. Cherry (2022)
*Beat Not Beat: An Anthology of California Poets Screwing
    on the Beat and Post-Beat Tradition* (2022)
*When There Are Nine: Poems Celebrating the Life and Achievements
    of Ruth Bader Ginsburg* (2022)
The Knife Thrower's Daughter, Terri Niccum (2022)
2 Revere Place, Aruni Wijesinghe (2022)
Here Go the Knives, Kelsey Bryan-Zwick (2022)
Trumpets in the Sky, Jerry Garcia (2022)
Threnody, Donna Hilbert (2022)
A Burning Lake of Paper Suns, Ellen Webre (2021)
Instructions for an Animal Body, Kelly Gray (2021)
Head *V* Heart: New & Selected Poems, Rob Sturma (2021)
*Sh!t Men Say to Me: A Poetry Anthology in Response
    to Toxic Masculinity* (2021)
Flower Grand First, Gustavo Hernandez (2021)
Everything is Radiant Between the Hates, Rich Ferguson (2020)
When the Pain Starts: Poetry as Sequential Art,
    Alan Passman (2020)

This Place Could Be Haunted If I Didn't Believe in Love,
    Lincoln McElwee (2020)
Impossible Thirst, Kathryn de Lancellotti (2020)
Lullabies for End Times, Jennifer Bradpiece (2020)
Crabgrass World, Robin Axworthy (2020)
Contortionist Tongue, Dania Ayah Alkhouli (2020)
The only thing that makes sense is to grow, Scott Ferry (2020)
Dead Letter Box, Terri Niccum (2019)
Tea and Subtitles: Selected Poems 1999-2019, Michael Miller (2019)
At the Table of the Unknown, Alexandra Umlas (2019)
The Book of Rabbits, Vince Trimboli (2019)
Everything I Write Is a Love Song to the World,
    David McIntire (2019)
Letters to the Leader, HanaLena Fennel (2019)
Darwin's Garden, Lee Rossi (2019)
Dark Ink: A Poetry Anthology Inspired by Horror (2018)
Drop and Dazzle, Peggy Dobreer (2018)
Junkie Wife, Alexis Rhone Fancher (2018)
The Moon, My Lover, My Mother, & the Dog,
    Daniel McGinn (2018)
Lullaby of Teeth: An Anthology of Southern California Poetry (2017)
Angels in Seven, Michael Miller (2016)
A Likely Story, Robbi Nester (2014)
Embers on the Stairs, Ruth Bavetta (2014)
The Green of Sunset, John Brantingham (2013)
The Savagery of Bone, Timothy Matthew Perez (2013)
The Silence of Doorways, Sharon Venezio (2013)
Cosmos: An Anthology of Southern California Poetry (2012)
Straws and Shadows, Irena Praitis (2012)
In the Lake of Your Bones, Peggy Dobreer (2012)
I Was Building Up to Something, Susan Davis (2011)
Hopeless Cases, Michael Kramer (2011)
One World, Gail Newman (2011)
What We Ache For, Eric Morago (2010)
Now and Then, Lee Mallory (2009)
Pop Art: An Anthology of Southern California Poetry (2009)
In the Heaven of Never Before, Carine Topal (2008)
A Wild Region, Kate Buckley (2008)
Carving in Bone: An Anthology of Orange County Poetry (2007)

Kindness from a Dark God, Ben Trigg (2007)
A Thin Strand of Lights, Ricki Mandeville (2006)
Sleepyhead Assassins, Mindy Nettifee (2006)
Tide Pools: An Anthology of Orange County Poetry (2006)
Lost American Nights: Lyrics & Poems, Michael Ubaldini (2006)

Patrons

Moon Tide Press would like to thank the following people for their support in helping publish the finest poetry from the Southern California region. To sign up as a patron, visit www.moontidepress.com or send an email to publisher@moontidepress.com.

Anonymous
Robin Axworthy
Conner Brenner
Nicole Connolly
Bill Cushing
Susan Davis
Kristen Baum DeBeasi
Peggy Dobreer
Kate Gale
Dennis Gowans
Alexis Rhone Fancher
HanaLena Fennel
Half Off Books & Brad T. Cox
Donna Hilbert
Jim & Vicky Hoggatt
Michael Kramer
Ron Koertge & Bianca Richards
Gary Jacobelly
Ray & Christi Lacoste
Jeffery Lewis
Zachary & Tammy Locklin
Lincoln McElwee
David McIntire
José Enrique Medina

Michael Miller &
Rachanee Srisavasdi
Michelle & Robert Miller
Ronny & Richard Morago
Terri Niccum
Andrew November
Jeremy Ra
Luke & Mia Salazar
Jennifer Smith
Roger Sponder
Andrew Turner
Rex Wilder
Mariano Zaro
Wes Bryan Zwick

Made in the USA
Middletown, DE
23 March 2025